Illustrations by Carles Marti

Scripture taken from the HOLY BIBLE, NEW INTERNATIONAL VERSION®. NIV®.
COPYRIGHT © 1973, 1978, 1984, 2011 by Biblica, Inc.®. Used by permission. All rights reserved worldwide.

The purchase of this coloring book grants you the rights to photocopy the contents for classroom use.
Notice: It is unlawful to copy these pages for resale purposes. Copy permission is for private use only.

Copyright © 2016 Warner Press, Inc. All rights reserved. Made in USA

305800210552

Jesus and His disciples took a trip to Jerusalem for the Passover celebration.

Jesus rode a donkey into the city. People were so happy to see Jesus! They waved palm branches and shouted, "HOSANNA!"

Jesus went to the temple and taught the people there every day.

The chief priests did not like Jesus. They planned to kill Him. One of Jesus' disciples named Judas agreed to help them.

The time came for the Passover meal. Jesus and His disciples ate and talked together.

After the meal, Jesus went to pray. Three of His disciples stayed nearby but kept falling asleep.

When Jesus was done praying, Judas walked up with some soldiers. The soldiers grabbed Jesus and took Him away.

Jesus was taken to Pilate, a leader in the city.
Pilate said, "Jesus has done nothing wrong."
But the crowd shouted, "Crucify Him!"

Jesus had to wear a crown of thorns. He had to carry His cross to Golgotha, which means "the place of the skull."

Jesus loved everyone so much that He died on the cross to save us from our sins.

A good, kind man took Jesus' body and put it in a tomb. A huge stone was rolled in front of the door.

Soon, Jesus' friends went to visit the tomb.
The stone was rolled away! Jesus was not there!

The women saw an angel. "Jesus is not here. He has risen!" the angel said. Jesus' friends were happy to know He was alive!

Later, Jesus appeared to His disciples. He showed them the nail scars on His hands and feet.

Then Jesus went to live in heaven.
If we believe and follow Jesus, we will live forever
with Him in heaven someday.

*God so loved the world that he gave his one and only Son,
that whoever believes in him shall not perish but have eternal life.*
John 3:16 (NIV)